# Living in the

# 1970s

Rosemary Rees & Judith Maguire

Heinemann Library,
an imprint of Heinemann Publishers (Oxford) Ltd,
Halley Court, Jordan Hill, Oxford, OX2 8EJ

OXFORD LONDON EDINBURGH
MADRID PARIS ATHENS BOLOGNA
MELBOURNE SYDNEY AUCKLAND
SINGAPORE TOKYO IBADAN
NAIROBI GABORONE HARARE
PORTSMOUTH NH (USA)

First published 1993
93 94 95 96 10 9 8 7 6 5 4 3 2 1

British Library Cataloguing in Publication Data
is available on request from the British Library.

ISBN 0 431 07216 7

Designed by Philip Parkhouse
Printed and bound in China

Acknowledgements
The authors and publisher would like to thank the following
for permission to reproduce photographs:
The Advertising Archives p. 20
Arcaid/Richard Einzig p. 6
Barnaby's Picture Library p. 5
BFI Stills p. 16
BBC p. 18
Collections/Brian Shuel p. 7
Camera Press pp. 23, 27
Robert Harding p. 30
Hulton-Deutsch Collection p. 22
Denise Kent p. 29
Judith Maguire p. 28
Robert Opie p. 17
Popperfoto p. 8
Syndication International Ltd p. 19
Topham Picture Source pp. 9, 12, 13, 14, 15
Stephen Vickers pp. 21, 25

Cover photograph: John Walmsley

# Contents

# Home 1

These two houses were built in the 1970s.
An old cottage had been knocked down.
These two houses were built in its place.
The houses had big rooms and big
windows.
Each house had a garage.
Each house also had a place to park a
car outside.

These teenagers were in their bedroom.
They had painted the bedroom walls in
very bright colours.
They liked staying in their bedroom,
listening to music and dancing.

# Home 2

In the 1970s, this kind of kitchen was new and different.

The lights in the kitchen are hidden behind the cupboards.

People wanted new kitchens to look like you had fun in them.

They did not want them to look like a place just for washing and cooking.

Most people did their shopping at the supermarket.

In 1971 money changed.

It was changed from 'old' money to the money we use today.

Some people found the new money hard to use.

Some shops had big charts to help them.

# School 1

These children learnt about new money at school.

Learning about old money was hard.

There were pennies, shillings and pounds.

Learning about new money was easier.

There are only pence and pounds.

These children went on an adventure
holiday with their school.
On this holiday they learnt to work well
with each other.
In the picture, the children have made a
raft from old oil drums.
They are ready to paddle down the river.

# School 2

These children went to playgroup.
Lots more playgroups started in the 1970s.
They went to playgroup when they were
3 or 4 years old.
Children often went to playgroups in the
morning. Playgroups were fun.

These children did a play at playgroup.
It was their Christmas play.
It was the story of Jesus.
The children had to remember to say their words. They also sang some songs.
Lots of mums and dads came to watch.
All the brothers and sisters came too.
Everybody clapped at the end.

# Work 1

In 1975, oil was found under the sea near Britain.

Oil rigs like this were built to get to the oil.

The oil was pumped from under the sea to the land.

Lots of oil was found, so oil was cheaper to buy. People were happy about this.

In 1973, the miners stopped digging for coal.

They wanted to be paid more money.

Coal was used to make electricity.

When the miners stopped digging for coal, electricity was not made.

Things that used electricity did not work.

People had to use candles or gas lamps in their houses.

# Work 2

The men in this picture were cutting the
wool from these sheep.
The men were sheep farmers.
They used electric cutters.
It was just like having a haircut. It didn't
hurt the sheep.

These people worked in an office.
Both men and women worked here.
In 1970, a new law was made.
It said men and women had to be paid
the same if they did the same job.
Some people thought this was good.
Some people thought women should be
paid less than men.

# Spare Time 1

This film was made in 1977.
Many people went to the cinema to watch it.
The film had lots of robots in it.
People thought there would be lots of robots in the future.
What films have you seen at the cinema?

This was the front page of a girl's magazine.

The magazine cost 4p.

Lots of girls read magazines like this.

This one had a picture of a pop singer on the front. Lots of girls liked him.

What kind of magazines do you like?

# Spare Time 2

This was a television programme called 'The Magic Roundabout'.

It was about a dog called Dougal and his friends.

Lots of children and grown-ups watched it. In the 1970s there were lots of television programmes made just for children.

This was a television programme called 'Tiswas'.

It was shown on Saturday mornings.

Sometimes the people on the programme did very silly things.

The man in black is 'The Phantom Flan Flinger'.

He threw flans at people.

# Spare Time 3

This is an advert for platform shoes.
Shoes like this were in fashion in the 1970s.
These shoes made people look taller.
It was hard to walk in these shoes.
What kind of shoes do you like to wear?

These people were at a party.

Look at their clothes.

All the women wore long dresses.

They were called maxi dresses.

Some of the men wore ties.

The ties were really wide.

They were called kipper ties.

# Holidays 1

This aeroplane was called Concorde.
It was very fast.
Concorde travelled faster than sound.
In the 1970s people started to go on
holiday by plane.
Not many people could fly in Concorde.
It cost too much money.

These people were on holiday in Spain.
They liked the sunshine.
Many people went to Spain for their
holiday.
They went there by plane.
It was faster to travel by plane.
Where do you like to go for your
holidays?

# Holidays 2

These two boys went on a farm holiday
in 1978.
They stayed in a cottage in Scotland.
It rained nearly all the time they were
there.
They did lots of walking in the hills.
They got very wet, but it was fun.

These people went on a camping holiday.
They took a tent to sleep in.
It rained so much they did not sleep in
the tent.
They had to find a caravan to sleep in.
They liked staying in a caravan.
It was dry.

# Special Days 1

In 1977 the Queen had her Silver Jubilee.
She had been queen for 25 years.
Lots of people had parties in the street.
Lots of special things were made to help
us remember the Silver Jubilee.
Mugs with a picture of the queen were
made. There were also special coins made.

This was Virginia Wade in 1977.
She was a very good tennis player.
Tennis is played at Wimbledon every year.
Virginia Wade won at Wimbledon in 1977.
Everyone wanted her to win.
People were happy that a British woman
had won.

# Special Days 2

This was a birthday party in the 1970s.
The party was had at home.
There was a special tea, with sausage
rolls, crisps and a big birthday cake.
Then all the children played games and
won prizes.
How are your birthday parties different?

This wedding was in 1977.
The bride and bridesmaids wore long dresses.
They carried flowers.
The men wore a flower on their jackets.
What do people wear at weddings today?

# Special Days 3

In 1972, there was a special exhibition in London.

People could see some very old treasures from Egypt.

One of the things you could see was this beautiful mask.

Lots of people wanted to see the Egyptian treasure, so you had to wait in line for a very long time.

# Time Line

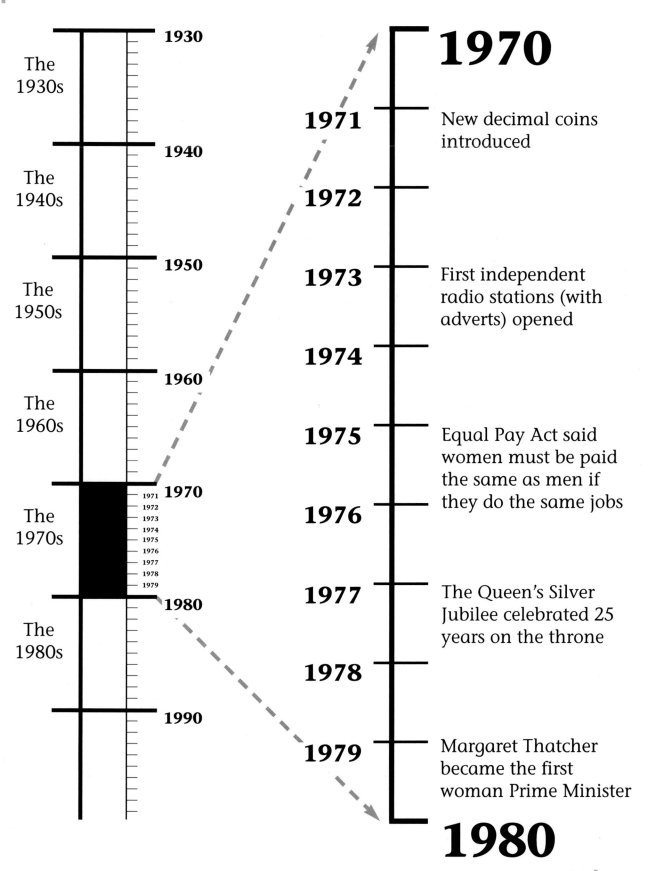

The 1930s

1930

The 1940s

1940

The 1950s

1950

The 1960s

1960

The 1970s

1970
1971
1972
1973
1974
1975
1976
1977
1978
1979

The 1980s

1980

1990

---

**1970**

**1971** New decimal coins introduced

**1972**

**1973** First independent radio stations (with adverts) opened

**1974**

**1975** Equal Pay Act said women must be paid the same as men if they do the same jobs

**1976**

**1977** The Queen's Silver Jubilee celebrated 25 years on the throne

**1978**

**1979** Margaret Thatcher became the first woman Prime Minister

**1980**

# Index